COOL CAREERS WITHOUT COLLEGE FOR
PEOPLE
WHO LOVE
TO MAKE
THINGS
GROW

COOL CAREERS WITHOUT COLLEGE FOR PEOPLE WHO LOVE TO MAKE THINGS GROW

MONIQUE BURNS

The Rosen Publishing Group, Inc.
New York

Published in 2004 by The Rosen Publishing Group, Inc.
29 East 21st Street, New York, NY 10010

Library of Congress Cataloging-in-Publication Data

Burns, Monique.
Cool careers without college for people who love to make things grow/ by Monique Burns.— 1st ed.
    p. cm. — (Cool careers without college)
Includes bibliographical references (p.   ).
Contents: Agricultural aviation pilot—Arborist—Botanical artist—Farm crop production technician—Farm equipment technician —Florist—Groundskeeper—Horticultural writer—Landscaper—Nursery grower—Organic farmer—Soil conservation technician.
ISBN 0-8239-3789-5 (library binding)
1. Plant specialists—Vocational guidance—Juvenile literature.
[1. Horticulture—Vocational guidance. 2. Vocational guidance.]
I. Title. II. Series.
SB50 .B87 2002
580'.23—dc21
                                                        2002011959

Manufactured in the United States of America

CONTENTS

Introduction 7

1 Agricultural Aviation
   Pilot 9

2 Arborist 20

3 Botanical Artist 31

4 Farm Crop Production
   Technician 42

5 Farm Equipment
   Technician 50

6 Florist 59

7 Groundskeeper 68

8 Horticultural Writer 81

9 Landscaper 94

10 Nursery Grower 106

11 Organic Farmer 115

12 Soil Conservation
    Technician 126

Glossary 136

Index 139

INTRODUCTION

When many people hear the word "career," they think of office work. They think of working indoors, away from the fresh air and sunshine. They think of handling paper and phone calls instead of interacting with their natural environment.

If you like working outdoors, or feel a special joy from watching plants and flowers grow, this book is for you. There are a variety of jobs that allow you to work with plants, and most do not require a college degree.

If you like growing vegetables, fruits, or herbs, you could become an organic farmer. If you want to combine your love of growing things with your love of art, you could become a florist, designing flower arrangements for special occasions. Or you could work as a botanical illustrator, drawing or painting pictures of plants and flowers for books and magazines.

If you like working outdoors to keep the natural environment in tip-top condition, consider a career as a landscaper or as a groundskeeper for a park, golf course, or even a private estate. If you're adventurous, you might work as an agricultural aircraft pilot, better known as a crop duster, flying your plane over farmers' fields, seeding crops, and spraying pesticides and fertilizers.

In this book, you'll find lots of information about the many cool careers for people who like the outdoors, nature, and growing things. Each chapter highlights a different career, provides information on what those workers actually do and how much money they earn, and discusses the pros and cons of each job. You will also find a list of books, magazines, and other resources to help you begin a rewarding career growing things and working with things that grow.

1

AGRICULTURAL AVIATION PILOT

If you love the natural landscape and crave adventure, a career as an agricultural aviation pilot might be just the ticket. Flying low, you'll spray fertilizers and other chemicals over fields and forests. You might even take aerial photographs of agricultural and wilderness areas to aid in conservation planning. Flying is risky, and exposure to

Flying low over a field of snap beans in Hebron, Maryland, this crop duster sprays a chemical that will get rid of the white mold that has plagued the bean crop for over a month.

chemicals can be dangerous. But for agricultural pilots, a life of freedom and excitement often makes up for potential hazards.

Description

There are many kinds of agricultural aviation pilots. Perhaps the best-known are aerial applicators, or "spray pilots." Once known as aerial crop dusters, or simply crop dusters, agricultural aviators fly small turboprop planes or helicopters over crops and orchards, spraying liquid fertilizers, herbicides, and pesticides. Some also spray chemical defoliators over cotton fields in the South to separate the cotton from its leaves. Very often, agricultural pilots drop seeds to sow fields or reforest wilderness areas.

Agricultural pilots also deliver cargo to and from farms, drop food over fields to feed livestock, and take aerial photographs of farms and forests. Some even help fight fires, preserving our natural environment by dumping water or fire retardants over burning fields and woodlands. Agricultural pilots can take on some or all of these tasks, depending on demand for their services as well as their training and interests.

Agricultural aviators live and work in about thirty states, in peaceful rural or suburban settings near farms and ranches. Most are found in California or the South, where the crop-growing season is the longest. Others work in the Northeast or West, where there are large forests and wilderness areas.

Working independently is a major perk of the job. Half of all agricultural aviators are self-employed. In addition to airborne tasks, these agricultural pilots care for their own aircraft, find and service clients, and keep business records. Other agricultural pilots are small business owners who often fly their own planes but who also hire and supervise other pilots, in addition to handling the business. The other half of all agricultural aviators work for large aerial applicator, or crop dusting, companies, or for the federal, state, or local

After Tropical Storm Gabrielle swept through Florida, it left behind pools of water that became breeding grounds for mosquitoes. This helicopter pilot prepares to blanket the pools with a pesticide from above.

government. Working alone or as part of a team, all agricultural pilots enjoy the joy and freedom of flight.

Piloting an agricultural aircraft is usually seasonal work. Spraying is done during the spring planting and summer growing seasons. In California and in the South, aviators work six to nine months. In the Northeast, work often lasts only two months. Some agricultural aviators move from one area to another to earn a full year's salary, beginning, say, in the South, where the growing season starts early, and working their way north.

Before spraying, pilots must post signs and notify residents and businesses so people and livestock can be moved from target areas. Some pilots mix the chemicals and load them into their planes. Others have ground crews to help.

Piloting any plane or helicopter can be hazardous, but agricultural aviators face special risks. Flying low to the ground, often just feet above crops, they encounter obstacles like trees, power lines, and houses. For protection, helmets, harnesses, safety belts, and fireproof flight suits are used. To prevent risks from chemicals, agricultural aviators wear protective masks and fireproof gloves.

Education and Training

Agricultural pilots must take a specialized flight training program plus log 500 hours of accident-free, precision, low-level flying to obtain a commercial pilot's license from the Federal Aviation Administration (FAA).

Aerial applicators also need specialized knowledge of the fertilizers, herbicides, and pesticides they use. You can learn about these chemicals through on-the-job training or by working with another spray pilot or for a large aerial applicator company. As an aerial applicator, you'll need a license from your state to handle and spray chemicals.

If you intend to do aerial photography, you'll need basic aerial photography skills. Experience is the best

How Chemical Fertilizers Were Born

Agricultural pilots often spray chemical fertilizers on crops. But who came up with the idea of using fertilizers to grow plants in the first place?

Fertilizers were discovered accidentally about 3,000 years ago. Early humans in Mesopotamia, a region of southwest Asia, noticed that when human excrement, animal manure, and vegetal waste fell on plants, they grew larger. The Egyptians also learned that silt from the Nile River, rich in nutrients from decaying fish and vegetal matter, made their crops grow better.

Under the ancient Romans, fertilization took a big step forward in 200 BC when Cato the Elder discovered that vegetables and many other plants grew better with nitrogen. Yet, surprisingly, fertilizer use suddenly stopped after the fall of the Roman Empire.

Finally, after ten centuries, fertilizer use began to make a slow comeback. In 1630, J. R. Glaubner, a German alchemist working in Amsterdam, Holland, discovered that potassium nitrate, or saltpeter, made an excellent fertilizer. At the time, few farmers took advantage of Glaubner's discovery, but today he is remembered as the inventor of chemical fertilizers.

In 1842, Englishman John B. Lawes founded the chemical fertilizer industry after developing a way to make superphosphate fertilizer by adding sulfuric acid to phosphate rocks. By the end of the nineteenth century, fertilizers came into fashion once again, and they've been helping farmers and plant growers ever since.

teacher, but a course in photography or aerial photography can help.

Salary

Work is seasonal, and the average mid-range salary for an agricultural aviator is $17,000. (Some pilots also earn a percentage of fees charged by their employer.) A pilot can earn as much as $35,000 a year by supplementing his or her income with other flying jobs during the off-season. Managers and owners of large aerial applicator companies usually earn more than self-employed pilots or employees.

Outlook

Between 1992 and 2005, employment opportunities for agricultural aviation pilots are expected to grow by 30 percent.

However, competition will be keen as military pilots retire from the U.S. armed forces and seek civilian jobs, and as commercial pilots lose their jobs due to changes in the airline industry since September 11, 2001.

FOR MORE INFORMATION

ORGANIZATIONS

Aerial Firefighting Industry Association
P.O. Box 523068
Springfield, VA 22152
(703) 644-6454
Web site: http://www.afia.com

AIR, Inc. (Aviation Information Resource)
3800 Camp Creek Parkway, Suite 18-100
Atlanta, GA 30331
(404) 592-6500
(800) AIR-APPS (247-2777)
Web site: http://www.jet-jobs.com

Canadian Aerial Applicators Association
P.O. Box 21085
Edmonton, AB T6R 2V4
Canada
(780) 413-0078
Web site: http://www.canadianaerialapplicators.com

Crop Life America (formerly National Agriculture Chemicals Association)
1156 15th Street NW, Suite 400
Washington, DC 20005
(202) 296-1585
Web site: http://www.croplifeamerica.org

Federal Aviation Administration (FAA)
AFS-20, Room 825
800 Independence Avenue SW
Washington, DC 20591
(202) 493-4876
Web site: http://www.faa.gov

The Fertilizer Institute
820 First Street NE
Washington, DC 20002
(202) 962-0490
Web site: http://www.tfi.org

National Agricultural Aviation Association (NAAA)
1005 E Street SE
Washington, DC 20003
(202) 546-5722
Web site: http://www.agaviation.org

National Coalition for Aviation Education
c/o TRW, Inc.
Attn: M. A. Thompson
1001 19th Street North
Arlington, VA 22209
Web site: http://www.aviationeducation.org

National Pest Management Association
8100 Oak Street
Dunn Loring, VA 22027
(703) 573-8330
Web site: http://www.pestworld.org

WEB SITES

Agricultural Aviation Online
http://www.ag-aviation-online.com

FAA Flight Standards Service
http://www1.faa.gov/avr/afs/index.cfm

BOOKS

AIR, Inc. *Collegiate Aviation Guide*. Atlanta, GA: AIR, Inc., 1999.

AIR, Inc. *The Ultimate Pilot Starter Kit*. Atlanta, GA: AIR, Inc., 2001.

Frazier, David. *Agricultural Pilot Flight Training Guide*. Blue Ridge Summit, PA: Tab Books, 1979.

Hoffsommer, Alan. *Agricultural Aviation*. New York: Sports Car Press, 1964.

PERIODICALS

AgAir Update
P.O. Box 1548
Perry, GA 31069
(912) 987-2250
Web site: http://www.agairupdate.com

Agricultural Aviation
National Agricultural Aviation Association (NAAA)
1005 E Street SE
Washington, DC 20003
(202) 546-5722
Web site: http://www.agaviation.org

Aircraft Maintenance Technology
Cygnus Business Media
1233 Janesville Avenue
Fort Atkinson, WI 53538
(920) 563-1699
Web site: http://www.amtonline.com

Aviation Maintenance
Phillips Business Information, L.L.C.
1201 Seven Locks Road, Suite 300
Potomac, MD 20854
(301) 340-7788, ext. 2265
Web site: http://www.aviationmx.com

General Aviation News
P.O. Box 39099
Lakewood, WA 98439
(253) 471-9888
Web site: http://www.generalaviationnews.com

MULTIMEDIA

So You Wanna Be an Agricultural Pilot? Package
Includes National Agricultural Aviation Association (NAAA) video, six-month subscription to *AgAir Update* magazine, and fact guide. From AIR, Inc.

2

ARBORIST

Did you like to climb trees as a child? Or maybe you enjoyed just sitting under their leafy branches. If you've always been interested in trees, consider a career as an arborist. You'll work with all kinds of trees, from small ornamentals to stately elms, oaks, and maples. Climbing high among branches, you'll prune the trees to maintain their health and beauty. Besides preserving an essential part of the landscape, your work will allow others to enjoy trees as much as you do!

Description

Arborists, also known as arboriculturists, are involved in all aspects of tree care. They inspect trees to make sure they are growing properly. They apply fertilizers and pesticides to spur growth or control bugs. Much of the job involves pruning trees, shaping them to improve their beauty, and clearing away dead or diseased branches that prevent growth, interfere with power lines, or pose hazards to pedestrians, motorists, or nearby homes and businesses. If a tree is damaged, an arborist uses special braces and cables to keep it upright and growing properly. If a tree dies or must be removed for a building project, an arborist cuts it down. Arborists also plant trees along city streets and in yards, gardens, parks, and forests.

Arborists usually work in urban or suburban settings. They might be employed by a city or town to care for trees in public areas, in parks, along sidewalks, and near buildings. They might work as part of a crew for a landscaping firm or tree-care company. Some arborists are self-employed and work alone or with a partner.

An arborist's work is rewarding but physically demanding. Most work is done outside during the warm spring and

The same tornado that swept away trailers in Ashland, Illinois, also took down many of the town's trees. These workers are helping to clear away the damaged limbs.

summer growing seasons, but arborists are exposed to all kinds of weather conditions, from blistering heat to chilling rain. Following tornadoes, hurricanes, or other natural disasters, arborists may be called to the scene immediately to remove damaged trees that have fallen on buildings or blocked roadways.

Arborists must be strong and healthy. Whether planting, fertilizing, pruning, or removing trees, they are constantly climbing, bending, or kneeling. Arborists also need a good sense of balance and must be comfortable working high above the ground in buckets, also called aerial lifts.

Strength and dexterity is necessary when handling equipment, too. Although arborists use shears, saws, pruners, and other hand tools, they also transport and handle heavy power equipment like chain saws, stump grinders, wood chippers, and sprayers used for applying chemical fertilizers and pesticides. Handheld power tools are especially hazardous when used high above the ground. Also, many chemicals are dangerous to handle or inhale. Although arborists use safety equipment like goggles, gloves, climbing ropes, and safety belts, or harnesses, they can suffer cuts, sprains, bruises, and falls.

Those arborists who don't actually want to prune, fertilize, and cut down trees often work as consulting arborists. A consulting arborist works with homeowners, landscapers, landscape architects, real-estate developers, and tree-service and landscaping companies. He or she advises them on the best trees to plant and how to care for them, as well as how to treat diseased, insect-infested, or damaged trees. If someone is hurt, or property is damaged by trees, consulting arborists work with insurance companies and the courts to provide expert testimony on the cause of the damage as well as its financial cost.

Education and Training

In high school, courses should include mathematics and science. If you intend to open your own company one day, you

An arborist prunes an almond tree in California. Pruning, the removal of unwanted limbs, can give the tree better balance, strengthen its main limbs, and make it more productive.

should include business courses as well. Most training occurs on the job. Working with an arborist, landscaper, or tree-service company on your afternoons or summers off can provide useful experience. Reading about tree care can also give you a lot of useful pointers.

Arborists do not need education beyond high school. Some choose to increase their job prospects by taking voluntary certification courses offered by the International Society of Arboriculture and other organizations. Graduates of two-year or four-year urban forestry programs that include courses in soil science, botany, dendrology, and arboriculture, as well as lab work and practical experience, are often qualified to open their own tree-service businesses.

Outlook

Although the U.S. Department of Labor does not maintain job statistics for arborists, jobs for those involved in the related professions of gardening and groundskeeping are expected to increase faster than the average for all occupations through 2005 because many people will be retiring. Arborists, in particular, are expected to do well because of the increased construction of new homes and businesses that will require their services. Also, as more and more people come to appreciate the beauty and usefulness of trees, demand for arborists will continue to grow.

Yearly earnings for arborists range from about $12,500 to $25,000. Foremen supervising crews of arborists can earn as much as $35,000. Salaries are also affected by where arborists work. In warm areas, arborists can work year-round, so salaries are higher. In areas that suffer frequent natural disasters, such as hurricanes and storms, arborists can earn additional money. Much depends on whether an arborist is self-employed or works for a large tree-service firm. These firms usually provide such benefits as medical insurance and paid vacation time.

Did You Know?

Trees are essential to our health and well-being. Besides beautifying the landscape, they perform these key functions:

- **Trees Provide Life-Giving Oxygen**

  People and animals need oxygen to breathe and stay alive. Trees give off oxygen as they absorb carbon dioxide. According to the U.S. Department of Agriculture (USDA), one acre of forest absorbs six tons of carbon dioxide and puts out four tons of oxygen. That's enough to meet the annual oxygen needs of eighteen people!

- **Trees Cool Temperatures and Lower Air-Conditioning Costs**

  Trees keep our environment cool and help cut down on energy use. The USDA estimates that the cooling effect of a young healthy tree is equivalent to ten room-size air conditioners operating twenty hours a day. The U.S. Forest Service says that the proper placement of trees around buildings can cut air-conditioning needs by 30 percent and save 20 to 50 percent in energy costs.

- **Trees Help Prevent Erosion**

  Trees protect our valuable farmlands and wood-lands, as well as our water supply, by preventing soil loss, or erosion. According to the U.S. Forest Service, the planting of trees means improved water quality because there is less erosion of lake-sides and riverbanks and runoff of sediments and chemicals into our waterways. Less runoff also means more recharging of the groundwater supply.

- **Trees Increase Property Values**

  Planting trees can improve a property's value. That means homeowners can sell their property for more money. Landscaping, especially with trees, can increase property values as much as 20 percent, according to the U.S. Forest Service.

FOR MORE INFORMATION

ORGANIZATIONS

American Association of Consulting Arborists (ASCA)
15245 Shady Grove Road, Suite 130
Rockville, MD 20850
(301) 947-0483
Web site: http://www.asca-consultants.org

American Forests
910 17th Street NW, Suite 600
Washington, DC 20006
(202) 955-4500
Web site: http://www.amfor.org

American Society for Horticultural Science (ASHS)
113 South West Street, Suite 200
Alexandria, VA 22314
(703) 836-4606
Web site: http://www.ashs.org

Forest Service
U.S. Department of Agriculture
P.O. Box 916090
Washington, DC 20090
(202) 205-8333
Web site: http://www.fs.fed.us

International Society of Arboriculture (ISA)
P.O. Box 3129
Champaign, IL 61826
(217) 355-9411
Web site: http://www.isa-arbor.com

National Arbor Day Foundation
100 Arbor Avenue
Nebraska City, NE 68410
(402) 474-5655
Web site: http://www.arborday.org

National Arborist Association (NAA)
3 Perimeter Road, Unit 1
Manchester, NH 03103
(800) 733-2622
(603) 314-5380
Web site: http://www.natlarb.com

Plant Amnesty
P.O. Box 15377
Seattle, WA 98115
(206) 783-9813
Web site: http://www.plantamnesty.com

Society of American Foresters (SAF)
5400 Grosvenor Lane
Bethesda, MD 20814
(301) 897-3690
Web site: http://www.safnet.org

WEB SITES

Arboriculture On-Line
http://isa-arbor.com

Arborist Site
http://www.arboristsite.com

ArborLearn Online Educational Workshops
http://www.arborlearn.org

Urban Forest: 50 Careers in Trees
http://www.urbanforest.org

BOOKS

Blair, Donald F., and Robert Shetterly. *Arborist Equipment: A Guide to the Tools and Equipment of Tree Maintenance*. Champaign, IL: International Society of Arboriculture, 1995.

Gilman, Dr. Edward E. *An Illustrated Guide to Pruning*. Florence, KY: Delmar Publishers, 1997.

Gilman, Dr. Edward E. *Trees for Urban and Suburban Landscapes*. Florence, KY: Delmar Publishers, 1997.

Harris, Richard Wilson, et al. *Arboriculture: Integrated Management of Landscape Trees, Shrubs, and Vines*. New York: Simon & Schuster, 1998.

James, N. D. G. *The Arboriculturist's Companion: A Guide to the Care of Trees*. 2nd ed. Boston, MA: Blackwell Press, 1990.

Pirone, Thomas P., et al. *Pirone's Tree Maintenance*. New York: Oxford University Press, 2000.

PERIODICALS
Tree Care Industry
3 Perimeter Road, Unit 1
Manchester, NH 03103
(800) 733-2622
(603) 314-5380
Web site: http://www.natlarb.com

NEWSLETTERS
The Tree Worker
3 Perimeter Road, Unit 1
Manchester, NH 03103
(800) 733-2622
(603) 314-5380
Web site: http://www.natlarb.com

VIDEOS
Pruning Horrors and Pruning Micro-Course, 2000. From Plant Amnesty.

BOTANICAL ARTIST

Drawing or painting pictures of plants and flowers can be just as much fun as planting and cultivating them! As a botanical artist, you'll combine your love of plants with your love of art. Closely observing plants and flowers, you'll note their intricate structures and wonderfully varied colors. Then you can bring these living works of art vividly to life at your drawing table or easel. Beyond the joy of creating beautiful objects, you give others the chance to enjoy and understand nature through your work.

Description

Botanical artists are visual artists who draw or paint intricately detailed pictures of plants, flowers, fruits, and herbs. They produce lifelike works that are correct right down to the smallest detail. When they paint flowers, for instance, they must depict the correct number of petals, the exact type of stem, and the precise colors that the flowers have in nature.

Some botanical artists work primarily as scientific illustrators or painters, producing works meant to be used in scientific or botanical textbooks or journals. These works are often extremely detailed and may focus on only a part of a plant, such as an interior or cross-sectional view of a stem.

Botanical artists may also be fine artists who produce paintings or drawings that are chiefly meant to be enjoyed for their aesthetic, or artistic, value. Although detail is important in these works, factors like composition are also

These artists observe their subjects in the Missouri Botanical Gardens. Flowers and other plants have always been a favorite subject of both realist and abstract painters.

key. Some botanical artists produce work for both artistic and scientific purposes.

Botanical artists often work as self-employed freelance illustrators or painters. As a botanical artist, your drawings or paintings of plants and flowers might appear in horticultural magazines or scientific journals, in books for consumers or scientists, and on Web sites for weekend gardeners or professional botanists. Your art might be used for marketing, to sell seeds or flowers in catalogs, or to illustrate packages and labels used to sell herbs, seeds, natural foods, and other plant-based products. Or you might simply produce works to sell to private collectors who love nature and appreciate beautiful art.

Botanical artists may specialize in a particular subject. They might draw or paint only flowers or plants or vegetables or herbs. There are even some botanical artists who paint only certain types of flowers or plants, such as orchids or roses. Others draw or paint a variety of plants and flowers, as well as insects, like caterpillars and ladybugs, that live in and around growing plants.

Spending a lot of time indoors, botanical artists work at their drawing tables or easels. But they frequently make field trips into the great outdoors to observe plants and flowers in their natural environment and to collect specimens. Some botanical illustrators cultivate their own gardens to insure they have just the right specimens on hand. Most botanical artists are familiar with techniques used to dry and preserve flowers and plants so they can save them for future study and use.

In addition to having a solid background in basic art techniques and a knowledge of plant structure, botanical artists have to communicate well with other people. They must be able to describe their work so they can get jobs, or commissions, and they must be able to listen closely to their clients to understand exactly what they want.

Education and Training

Botanical artists need training in art as well as a knowledge of plant structure. Take art, drafting, biology, and botany courses in high school. If your city has a specialized high school for visual artists, plan to attend.

To gain hands-on experience, draw and paint pictures of flowers and plants on your own. There are many books that teach basic techniques in various media, including pencil, pen and ink, watercolors, and acrylic and oil paints. Spend time in home gardens, botanical gardens, nature preserves, and other areas where you can sketch flowers and plants, or collect specimens to study and work from when you get home.

After high school, sign up for art classes or attend a two-year art school that offers a program in botanical illustration.

Our New Guide

Autumn 1894

OTAHEITE ORANGE. See third cover page.

BULBS, ROSES AND PLANTS.

The Dingee & Conard Co.,

WEST GROVE, PA.

During this time, you can develop a portfolio of your work to show prospective clients or employers. Because of the level of detail required in their works, botanical artists generally do not use computer drawing software, but they sometimes use the Photoshop or Painter programs, along with scanners, to reproduce their work. You also should know how to use computer e-mail and word processing to communicate with clients.

Outlook

Employment for visual artists is expected to grow at a faster rate than the average for all other occupations through 2008. But competition for freelance work or full-time positions will continue to be stiff since so many people are attracted to artistic fields.

Botanical artists may experience an increased demand for their services as more and more people become interested in gardening and natural foods, and as more magazines, books, gardening companies, and natural-foods companies are developed to meet their needs. Increased numbers of gardening and other horticultural Web sites should also mean more jobs for botanical artists.

Botanical artists have long produced illustrations that grace the covers of nursery catalogues, like this one from 1894. Others paint canvases that hang in the homes of art collectors.

About 60 percent of all visual artists are self-employed freelancers, and many botanical artists are self-employed. Pay rates for freelancers vary. Large advertising firms and large companies generally pay the most. They are followed by large book publishers and national magazines with large circulations. Small companies and small publishing houses usually pay the least. A freelancer can earn any-where from $10,000 to $100,000 or more annually, depend-ing on what his or her clients pay and the number of works created each year.

Profile

CAROL BOLT, BOTANICAL ARTIST

Carol Bolt, a member of the American Society of Botanical Artists (ASBA), lives and works in New York City. In addition to creating botanical paintings for collec-tors, she produces works that have appeared in books and on packaging for products by designer Ralph Lauren. Bolt also paints still lifes, landscapes, and portraits.

HOW DID YOU BECOME INTERESTED IN BOTANICAL ART?

I always wanted to be an artist. I used to draw horses a lot and funny pictures of people. I made my first sale when I was five. I had lessons from the time I was seven, and my mother took me to museums about twice a month. After graduating from the California Institute of the Arts, I painted still lifes, landscapes, and portraits. I began working in botanical art about thirty years ago.

WHAT TRAINING SHOULD A BOTANICAL ARTIST HAVE?

You don't need a degree to be a botanical artist, but you should take at least a two-year course in art school so you have basic art skills. Then you should take specialized courses in botanical art. In New York, the Horticultural Society of New York, the Brooklyn Botanic Garden, and the New York Botanical Garden give classes. There are classes elsewhere in the country as well. They can be found at Chicago's Morton Arboretum; at the Museum of the Desert in Tucson, Arizona; at the Denver Botanic Garden in Colorado; and at the Ringling Art School in Sarasota, Florida, for instance. Many ASBA members around the country also give courses.

WHAT SPECIAL SKILLS DOES A BOTANICAL ARTIST NEED?

Aside from having basic art skills, a botanical artist must have really good observation skills. You need a really good eye for proportion, detail, and color. And you need a lot of patience so you can capture all those many details in your drawing or painting.

FOR MORE INFORMATION

ORGANIZATIONS

American Society of Botanical Artists (ASBA)
47 Fifth Avenue
New York, NY 10003
(866) 691-9080 (toll free in U.S.)
(212) 691-9080
e-mail: cbolt@nyc.rr.com
Web site: http://huntbot.andrew.cmu.edu/ASBA/ASBotArtists.html

Guild of Natural Science Illustrators
P.O. Box 652
Ben Franklin Station
Washington, DC 20044
(301) 309-1514
Web site: http://www.gnsi.org

The National Association of Schools of Art and Design
11250 Roger Bacon Drive, Suite 21
Reston, VA 20190
(703) 437-0700
Web site: http://www.arts-accredit.org

WEB SITES

The Society of Botanical Artists
http://www.soc-botanical-artists.org

Hunt Institute for Botanical Documentation (Carnegie Mellon University)
http://huntbot.andrew.cmu.edu

BOOKS

Blunt, Wilfred, and William T. Stearn, eds. *The Art of Botanical Illustration*. New York: Dover Publications, 1994.

Hodges, Elaine R. S., ed. *The Guild Handbook of Scientific Illustration*. New York: John Wiley & Sons, 2003.

Sherwood, Shirley, and Victoria Matthews, eds. *Contemporary Botanical Artists: The Shirley Sherwood Collection*. London, England: Ewidenfeld & Nicolson, 1996.

Sherwood, Shirley. *A Passion for Plants*. New York: Sterling Publishing Co., 2001.

West, Keith R. *How to Draw Plants: The Techniques of Botanical Illustration*. Portland, OR: Timber Press, 1996.

West, Keith R. *Painting Plant Portraits: A Step-by-Step Guide*. Portland, OR: Timber Press, 1997.

Wunderlich, Eleanor B. *Botanical Illustration in Watercolor*. New York: Watson-Guptill, 1996.

Zuk, Judith D., and Christopher Brickell. *American Horticultural Society A-Z Encyclopedia of Garden Plants*. New York: DK Publishing, 1997.

4

FARM CROP PRODUCTION TECHNICIAN

You love farming but don't actually want to own a farm. Working as a farm crop production technician can be equally rewarding! You'll be out in the open air, visiting farms, and making seed, soil, and equipment recommendations to help farmers grow better crops. As a troubleshooter, you'll spring into action if crops are not growing as planned or if a natural disaster strikes. Being a farm crop production technician just might be the next best thing to being a farmer!

Description

Farm crop production technicians help farmers increase their crop yields. They are involved in every aspect of crop production and management, from choosing and planting seeds to harvesting and bringing crops to market. Farm crop production technicians don't do the actual farmwork, but they're out in the field, analyzing soil conditions, suggesting fertilizers to promote growth, and recommending ways to control disease and insects. Farm crop production technicians make studies of farmers' yields and monitor crops throughout their growth to insure they meet expectations. They oversee harvests. Sometimes, they suggest alternative uses for crops to help farmers earn more or cope with a surplus. Experienced farm crop production technicians might even help manage the farm's business, making recommendations on hiring workers, choosing machinery, and handling finances.

Some farm crop production technicians handle all aspects of crop production, from planting to harvesting and processing. Others specialize in a particular area, such as soil or pest management. Some farm crop production technicians

If a crop is going to produce a good yield, it has to be kept healthy when it is still in the early stages of its growth. This crop production technician inspects some young tomatoes.

work with diversified farms that produce a variety of crops, such as wheat, corn, fruit, and vegetables. Others work with specialized farms that grow only one or two crops. These include farms that produce seeds for commercial seed companies, orchards where fruit trees are cultivated, and vineyards that produce grapes for winemaking.

Farm crop production technicians can work directly with farmers as self-employed independent contractors. But most are employed by companies that support agriculture, including feed and supply companies and farm equipment sales and service companies. They also work for food-processing companies whose profits are directly affected by the production of farmers who supply their crops.

These farm crop production technicians work out in the field and may be exposed to extreme weather conditions. During planting and harvesting seasons, they often work long hours to insure all goes according to plan. If a natural disaster strikes, such as a hurricane or flood, or a premature frost or sudden insect infestation, technicians might work round the clock until the problem is solved.

Some farm crop production technicians work primarily indoors. They are employed in government laboratories or for companies involved in nutrition research or quality control. They might work in food-processing plants, overseeing the testing, grading, packaging, and transportation of processed crops.

Farm crop production technicians must be comfortable communicating with other people, particularly farmers. They often have to explain, in a sympathetic way, why a farmer's methods aren't working. They also must explain scientific or high-tech procedures in a clear, understandable manner.

Being well-organized is important for farm crop production technicians because many operations involved in crop production must occur at just the right times. They should also have a talent for problem solving. Being even tempered

Chickpeas being packaged by a machine are inspected by this farm crop production technician. The packages that he looks at will be put on trucks and distributed throughout the country.

is also helpful since crops are affected by many unseen factors, including the weather. When things don't go according to plan, you have to remain cool, calm, and collected as you focus on just the right solution.

Education and Training

Growing up on a farm is a good start, but it is not necessary. You also can get valuable experience by joining a 4-H Club or the National FFA Organization (once known as Future Farmers of America). In high school, take courses in biology and the earth sciences, mathematics, and communications. If possible, attend a vocational school and take agriculture courses.

After high school, training at a two-year technical or business college is usually necessary. You can take courses while working on a farm or at a company involved in crop production. Farm crop production technicians are not required to be licensed or certified. However, if you want to grade or inspect crops for the local, state or federal government, you have to pass an examination.

Salary

Earnings for farm crop production technicians vary, but average yearly salaries are in the $18,000 to $30,000 range. Technicians working off the farm generally earn more than technicians working on farms. But on-site farm crop production technicians may receive food and housing benefits. Those working in areas like California, Minnesota, and Iowa generally make more money than those working in the Northeast. Whether you receive medical or vacation benefits depends on who employs you.

Outlook

Jobs for farm crop production technicians are expected to increase at the average rate for all other occupations.

FOR MORE INFORMATION

ORGANIZATIONS

Crop Science Society of America
677 South Segoe Road
Madison, WI 53711
(608) 273-8080
Web site: http://www.crops.org

4-H
Stop 2225
1400 Independence Avenue SW
Washington, DC 20250
(202) 720-2908
Web site: http://www.4h-usa.org

National Alliance of Independent Crop Consultants (NAICC)
349 East Nolley Drive
Collierville, TN 38017
(901) 861-0511
Web site: http://www.naicc.org

National FFA Center (formerly Future Farmers of America)
6060 FFA Drive
P.O. Box 68960
Indianapolis, IN 46268
(317) 802-6060
Web site: http://www.ffa.org

U.S. Department of Agriculture
14th Street and Independence SW
Washington, DC 20250

(202) 720-2791
Web site: http://www.usda.gov

WEB SITES

Agriculture Web
http://www.agweb.com

BOOKS

Donnelly, Kevin. *Crop Production*. Dubuque, IA: Kendall/Hunt Publishing Co., 1998.

Ferguson Publishing. *Ferguson's Careers in Focus/Agriculture.* Chicago, IL: Ferguson Publishing Co., 2000.

Smith, C. Wayne. *Crop Production: Evolution, History, and Technology.* New York: John Wiley & Sons, 1995.

Vorst, James J. *Crop Production.* 5th ed. Champaign, IL: Stipes Publishing, 1998.

PERIODICALS

CPM, Crop Production Magazine
Media Products, Inc./United Agri Products
P.O. Box 1-B
Eugene, OR 97440
(800) 874-3276
(541) 687-2315
Web site: http://www.CPMMagazine.com

Farm Journal: The Magazine of American Agriculture
1818 Market Street, 31st Floor
Philadelphia, PA 19103
Web site: http://www.agweb.com

5

FARM EQUIPMENT TECHNICIAN

Have you always enjoyed fixing things? Or just taking things apart and putting them back together? If you like working with your hands and are fascinated by how things work, consider a job as a farm equipment technician. You'll repair and maintain machines used in every aspect of farming, from planting and cultivating to harvesting and storing. Though most work is indoors, you'll have many chances to get out in the field to make repairs, and sometimes even drive the big machines yourself!

Description

Farm equipment technicians, also known as agricultural equipment technicians, maintain and repair farm equipment used for a variety of tasks, including planting, cultivating, harvesting, storing, and processing crops. They work on irrigation equipment used to water fields.

Farm equipment technicians first observe, then test machines, using electronic testing devices to see what's gone wrong. In some cases, they have to take apart machines to figure out the problem.

Once they have uncovered the problem, they have to fix it. As a farm equipment technician, you'll use a variety of hand tools, such as screwdrivers, wrenches, and pliers. You'll also use power tools, including welding equipment and saws. To reconstruct a machine part or do body-work repairs, you might use drill presses, lathes, and woodworking machines.

Farm equipment technicians also perform preventative maintenance tasks. They oil or lubricate the moving parts of farm machines, and clean and adjust parts to keep things running smoothly. When the growing and harvesting seasons are over, they overhaul farm machines, checking and adjusting them so they'll be ready for the next crops.

This combine can't go out into the field until this farm equipment technician fixes its hydraulic line. Farms are often run on a very strict schedule and cannot afford to have work held up by faulty machinery.

Farm equipment technicians work throughout the United States, mainly in rural farming areas. But they also work in suburban areas where homeowners, gardeners, and landscapers need riding mowers and other equipment repaired.

Most farm equipment technicians work in the service departments of equipment dealerships. Some farm equipment technicians are hired by large farms. Other farm equipment technicians work for independent shops that specialize in maintaining farm equipment. Some farm equipment technicians are self-employed and run their own shops.

In large shops and service departments, farm equipment technicians usually specialize. Some might work on tractors and other farm vehicles that have gas-powered engines, while others might work only on diesel-powered farm vehicles. Some might work only on air-conditioning systems used in the cabs of trucks, combines, and big tractors.

Most of the time, farmers bring machinery to the shop or service department, and work is done indoors. But if it's the busy planting or harvesting season, and a machine suddenly breaks down, farm equipment technicians will go out to the field to inspect and repair machinery.

Some technicians, known as farm machinery set-up mechanics, work for companies that manufacture farm equipment. They deliver machinery to farms, then uncrate, assemble, and adjust it.

There are also farm equipment technicians—known as equipment manufacturing technicians, agricultural engineering technicians, and agricultural equipment test technicians—who help design and test farm equipment for manufacturers. They may also be employed by the U.S. Department of Agriculture and the Agriculture Research Service. Some farm equipment technicians supervise plant operations for manufacturers.

Tools of the Trade

Here are just a handful of the many machines used on farms:

Blower A machine used to blow hay up a pipe and into a silo for storage.

Combine A large, self-propelled machine used to harvest grain crops. It cuts grain, separates it from the straw, leaves the straw in neat rows, and stores the grain in a bin. Different attachments, or heads, are used to harvest different types of grain. For instance, a reel-type head is used for wheat, and a corn head is used for corn.

Corn harvester A machine that cuts, chops, and blows corn into wagons.

Drill A device that is pulled behind a tractor and seeds fields. It makes long grooves in the soil, drops seed into them, then covers the seeds with soil.

Hay baler A machine that gathers up dry hay into big rectangular or round bundles called bales.

Tractor The main farm vehicle used in the fields. Many different types of farm equipment used for planting, mowing, and harvesting can be attached to it and pulled through the fields.

Farm equipment technicians can also use their knowledge of agricultural machines to work as salespeople and sales managers for manufacturers who sell their equipment to local dealerships, or for the dealerships themselves.

Education and Training

In high school, take courses in mathematics, earth sciences, mechanical drawing, and shop. If you can, attend a vocational school and take electronics courses. Look for after-school work in the service department of a farm equipment manufacturing company or dealership, or with a self-employed technician. Working for an automobile mechanic can also be helpful, even if you want to repair farm vehicles.

Although on-the-job training is useful, as farm equipment becomes more and more complex and computerized, technicians find they need more advanced schooling. Many agriculture colleges and junior colleges in rural areas offer two-year programs that include courses in agriculture, agricultural equipment, and practical engineering. Some include summer internships as part of their program to give students hands-on experience.

Outlook

Jobs for farm equipment technicians are expected to increase as fast as the average for all other occupations. The greatest demand will be for technicians trained in repairing modern machinery using computers and electronics.

Annual salaries for farm equipment technicians who work for large equipment manufacturers or dealerships range from about $15,000 to $32,000. Supervisors and managers can earn an average of $42,000. Those who work for the federal government earn about $23,000 to $30,000, but opportunities for advancement are offered regularly. Farm equipment technicians working as salespeople often receive commissions in addition to their base salaries. Those who work on farms may receive room and board in addition to a salary. Farm equipment technicians who work for large companies or the federal government receive medical benefits, paid vacation time, and retirement packages.

FOR MORE INFORMATION

ASSOCIATIONS

Association of Equipment Management Professionals (formerly The Equipment Maintenance Council)
P.O. Box 1368
Glenwood Springs, CO 81602
(970) 384-0510
Web site: http://www.equipment.org

Association of Equipment Manufacturers
10 South Riverside Plaza
Chicago, IL 60606
(866) AEM-0442
(312) 321-1470
Web site: http://www.aem.org

Farm Equipment Manufacturers Association (FEMA)
1000 Executive Parkway, Suite 100
St. Louis, MO 63141
(314) 878-2304
Web site: http://www.farmequip.org

National Automotive Technicians Education Foundation (NATEF)
101 Blue Seal Drive, Suite 101
Leesburg, VA 20175
(703) 669-6650
Web site: http://www.natef.org

National FFA Organization (formerly known as Future Farmers of America)
6060 FFA Drive
P.O. Box 68960
Indianapolis, IN 46268
(317) 802-6060
Web site: http://www.ffa.org

North American Equipment Dealers Association
1195 Smizer Mill Road
Fenton, MO 63026
(636) 349-5000
Web site: http://www.naeda.com

WEB SITES

Farmnet Farm Machinery
http://www.farmnet.com.au

BOOKS

Brunn, Erik A., and Buzzy Keith. *Heavy Equipment: Giant Machines That Crush, Dig, Dredge, Drill, Excavate, Grade, Haul, Pave, Pulvertize, Pump, Push, Pull, Roll, Stack, Thresh and Transport Big Things*. New York: BD&L Publishing, 1997.

Carroll, John. *The World Encyclopedia of Tractors and Farm Machinery*. New York: Anness Publishing, 2002.

Deere, John. *The Operation, Care, and Repair of Farm Machinery: Practical Hints for Handy Men*. Guilford, CT: Globe Pequot Press, 2000.

Ramsower, Harry C. *Farm Equipment and How to Use It*. New York: Lyons Press, 2001.

Richards, Jon. *Farm Machines*. Brookfield, CT: Millbrook Press, 1999.

Whiley, Peter. *Farm Machinery Maintenance*. Woburn, MA: Butterworth-Heinemann, 1997.

PERIODICALS

Farm Equipment
Cygnus Publishing
1233 Janesville Avenue
Ft. Atkinson, WI 53538
Web site: http://www.farm-equipment.com

Farm Show
Johnson Building
P.O. Box 1029
Lakeville, MN 55044
(800) 834-9665
Web site: http://www.farmshow.com

6

FLORIST

Are you captivated by the beauty of plants and flowers? Do you have a flair for arranging plants and flowers in ways that enhance their natural beauty or that express a particular mood or feeling? Do you have artistic talent and do you enjoy working with your hands? Do you like interacting closely with other people? If you answered yes, you'd

or celebration. Many florists visit the setting to insure that their arrangements will blend well with the décor.

Flowers and arrangements often mark joyous occasions like birthdays and weddings, or holidays like Thanksgiving, Christmas, and Valentine's Day. At these times, conversations with customers are usually upbeat and lively. But there are also sad occasions, like illnesses and funerals, when you must have the sensitivity and patience to deal with worried or grieving friends and relatives.

Since many florists run their own shops, they need good time-management skills and discipline to insure their creations are completed and delivered on time. They also need business skills to keep track of inventory, buy flowers and plants from wholesale suppliers, price items, and hire and train workers. In addition to serving local customers, florists often work with international floral wire services, such as FTD and Tele-Flora. These services will contact you by telephone or e-mail and ask you to re-create set arrangements from their catalogs for a set price. Such services are used when out-of-town customers want to send flowers to people in your area. Other florists work in similar ways for floral services on the Web.

Education and Training

If you want to be a florist, take high-school courses in art and design, biology and botany, English and communications, and accounting, business, and computers. Try to

Flowers Through the Ages

Early civilizations used flowers for decoration, for religious observances, and for celebrations. The ancient Egyptians put flowers in their hair and clothing, and placed flower arrangements on the altars of gods and goddesses. Ancient Greeks used wreaths for decoration, as gifts, and to honor athletes and other heroes. Today, winning marathon runners are still crowned with fragrant laurel wreaths, and Olympic champions receive large floral bouquets.

Through the centuries, people continued to use flowers. In the nineteenth century, flowers and gardening soared in popularity. Young women learned flower arranging, as well as music, sewing, and other skills. They wore small bouquets, called nosegays, tucked into their dresses in containers called bosom bottles. Or they carried small glass, pearl, or ivory vases known as posy holders.

In the 1950s, free-form expression influenced by the sixth-century style of Japanese arrangements called ikebana became popular. These arrangements used driftwood and even figurines. Today, florists use many styles, including traditional, free form, and ikebana, in their creations.

Special orders and large-scale arrangements often have to be tailored to a customer's specifications, although many customers will ask for the florist's recommendations.

attend a specialized vocational high school that offers courses in floriculture and flower design. Read books about flower arranging and experiment at home using flowers and plants to make arrangements and wreaths for special occasions.

On-the-job training is especially useful. Try to get an after-school job with a local florist during holidays or summers off. While in school or after graduation, your first jobs may involve caring for and selling cut flowers or delivering arrangements, but you can learn much about floral design and about the business by watching an experienced florist at work. You may even be allowed to design simple arrangements yourself! To progress more quickly in the field, consider taking floriculture and business courses after high school that will enable you to start as a floral designer or to open your own shop.

Salary

Salaries for florists vary according to experience and place of employment. A first-year florist earns an average of $6.15 an hour, while one with three years' experience can earn $8.39 an hour. Managers and supervisors earn about $24,000 a year, and owners of large florist shops can earn $30,000 a year or more. Florists on the East and West Coasts generally earn more than those elsewhere in the United States. Some shops offer medical and vacation benefits.

Outlook

With consumers' increased interest in using flowers and plants to beautify their surroundings, it's expected that demand for florists will remain strong. Most opportunities exist in retail florist shops, where florists work as self-employed owners or as employees. Nurseries and garden centers, as well as large hotels and resorts, may also employ florists. Increasingly, large supermarkets are hiring florists and managers to sell cut flowers and plants, and to design arrangements. Florists can also work for large wholesale florist operations, where they care for cut flowers and plants, and supervise delivery of shipments, rather than design arrangements.

FOR MORE INFORMATION

ORGANIZATIONS

The American Institute of Floral Designers
720 Light Street
Baltimore, MD 21230
(410) 752-3318
Web site: http://www.aifd.org

Society of American Florists
1601 Duke Street
Alexandria, VA 22314
(703) 836-8700
Web site: http://www.safnow.org

Wholesale Florist and Florist Supplier Association
Old Solomons Island Road, Suite 302
Annapolis, MD 21401
(888) 289-3372
(410) 573-0400
Web site: http://www.wffsa.org

BOOKS

Bourne, H. *The Florist Manual.* Bedford, MA: Applewood Books, 2000.

Hessayon, David G. *The Flower Arranging Expert.* New York: Expert Books, 1994.

Pfahl, Peter B. *The Retail Florist Business.* Danville, IL: Interstate Publishers, 1994.

Turner, Kenneth. *Flower Style: The Art of Floral Design and Decoration.* New York: Sterling Publishing Co., 2000.

PERIODICALS

The Florist
The FTD Association
33031 Schoolcraft Road
Livonia, MI 48150
(800) 383-4383
Web site: http://www.ftd.com

7

GROUNDSKEEPER

If you enjoy seeing manicured lawns and athletic fields stretching into the distance, consider a career as a groundskeeper. You'll keep lawns and plantings in tip-top condition, and you'll maintain walks, driveways, parking lots, and benches. Out in the open air, you'll use all kinds of hand and power tools. Besides beautifying the landscape, you'll help other people enjoy it, whether they're playing golf, baseball, or football, picnicking with the family, or just strolling and taking in the scenery.

Description

Groundskeepers maintain a variety of outdoor green spaces, including athletic fields and golf courses, parks and playgrounds, resorts and theme parks, college campuses and cemeteries, and office and residential complexes. Much of the work involves seeding, watering, fertilizing, trimming, and mowing lawns. Working throughout the year, groundskeepers rake leaves in the fall and clear away snow in the winter. They also clear away and dispose of litter.

To care for athletic fields, groundskeepers mark out boundaries and paint turf with team logos. Those who maintain artificial turf for athletic fields vacuum, wash, and disinfect it to prevent the spread of bacteria, and even replace it from time to time.

Groundskeepers may maintain plantings, including trees and shrubs, as well as water and fertilize them. Some even spray pesticides. In addition to caring for lawns and landscapes, groundskeepers often maintain sidewalks, parking lots, benches, and fences as well as fountains and pools. They also keep the exteriors of buildings freshly painted. Those groundskeepers, known as greenskeepers, who work

These groundskeepers meticulously groom the Bethpage State Park's golf course. A poorly maintained golf course can disrupt play.

for golf courses, keep outdoor tee markers, ball washers, benches, and canopies in good repair.

Groundskeepers who work at cemeteries also have special duties, such as digging graves (often using an excavating machine called a backhoe), positioning casket-lowering devices, erecting canopies over burial sites, and setting up folding chairs for graveside ceremonies.

Employed throughout the United States, most groundskeepers work full-time, particularly in regions with year-round warm weather. Others are hired part-time.

Although some groundskeepers work alone and have full responsibility for a park or other outdoor area, most of them hire and supervise workers during the busy spring and summer growing seasons. Other groundskeepers supervise or work as part of a crew of workers.

Groundskeeping, like landscaping, can be physically demanding and is performed in all kinds of weather. Work often starts in the early morning, particularly at golf courses and other recreational facilities that will be used throughout the day. Hand tools such as shovels, rakes, and leaf blowers are used, along with heavy power tools like chain saws, brush cutters, and snowblowers. Power lawn mowers and small tractors are often used, too. Most groundskeepers are expected to maintain, and sometimes repair, their tools and vehicles.

When maintaining athletic fields, particularly golf-course greens, groundskeepers must have knowledge of various kinds of grass, or turf, how each type grows, and how each type reacts when played upon in various kinds of weather. Because turf has such a big effect on how golf balls roll, greenskeepers must be especially mindful of the turf. They'll even move the holes on a putting green, from time to time, to insure the turf wears evenly!

In addition to knowing how to maintain the lawns, or turf, and plantings, those who become head groundskeepers, or superintendents, must be able to communicate well with the workers they supervise.

Education and Training

Most groundskeepers learn on the job. In high school, take courses in biology and the earth sciences, as well as English and communications. If you can, attend an agricultural or technical high school that offers landscaping courses. After school and during your summers off, work part-time for a groundskeeper or landscaper.

After graduation, work as a groundskeeper, or as part of a groundskeeping crew. If you want to work as a specialized groundskeeper for a golf course or athletic field, it's helpful to take a two-year course at an agricultural or junior college that provides courses in soil science and turf-grass management.

Certification is not necessary, but several organizations, including the Professional Grounds Management Society (PGMS) and the Associated Landscape Contractors of America (ALCA), offer certification programs that can lead to higher-paying jobs.

Outlook

Jobs for groundskeepers are expected to grow faster than the average for all other occupations through 2010. There is high turnover in the field as part-time workers leave to seek full-time employment in their chosen careers, or as people seek jobs in higher-paying occupations. In addition, there will be a continuing need for groundskeepers with increased construction of new home and office complexes as well as recreational facilities like golf courses, baseball and football fields, resorts, and theme parks.

Groundskeeping positions do not pay a great deal, especially in the beginning. Entry-level workers can expect to earn about $8 an hour, while supervisors earn about $15 an hour. Those working in local government usually earn more. If you are specialized in turf-grass management and work for a golf course, or a college or professional athletic facility, you can earn even more.

Profile

KEVIN WILES, SUPERINTENDENT OF THE OCEAN COURSE AT KIAWAH ISLAND RESORTS

Kevin Wiles is superintendent, or head greenskeeper, of the world-famous Ocean Course at Kiawah Island Resorts near Charleston, South Carolina. Although he does some of the greenskeeping work himself, he also supervises a crew of twenty-five greenskeeping workers year-round and sixty-five workers in summer.

These groundskeepers groom the Keeneland Racetrack in preparation for the first race of the evening. Racetrack dirt must be kept smooth and free of rocks to protect the horses that race on it.

HOW DID YOU GET INVOLVED IN GREENSKEEPING?

My father played golf and got me started in the game. He worked at the Concord Hotel in Monticello, New York, and during my summers off from high school, I did greenskeeping there. After high school, I attended Morrisville Agricultural & Technical College where I studied auto mechanics. Knowing how to repair and maintain vehicles came in handy on my early groundskeeping jobs.

But I always liked turf. So I attended the Abraham Baldwin College in Tifton, Georgia, for two years and took courses in landscaping and turf-grass management. I worked at a few golf courses in Savannah, Georgia, then moved to Charleston, South Carolina, where I worked for three or four years at the Links at Stono Ferry. I've been a superintendent for about eighteen years. I came to the Kiawah Island Resorts about five years ago, and worked at the resorts' Oak Point and Cougar Point courses before taking on the Ocean Course.

HOW IMPORTANT IS TURF-MANAGEMENT FOR A GREENSKEEPER?

You have to really understand the soils and the various kinds of turf. While I was at Morrisville Agricultural & Tech, I worked for two top plant geneticists, who developed a new turf that is still used on golf courses up north. In addition to schooling, you need four or five years of practical experience. You have to play a golf course, or at least walk it, so you see how different kinds of turf behave under different conditions. You have to experience turf in the real world. You have to say, why is this turf dying, what are the variables, before you can say, let's spray this fertilizer or that pesticide.

DO YOU FACE ANY SPECIAL CHALLENGES MAINTAINING THE OCEAN COURSE?

Well, because the Ocean Course is situated right on the ocean, if there's heavy wind or rain, the entire course melts down, and you have to replace the turf or rebuild portions.

FOR MORE INFORMATION

ASSOCIATIONS

American Institute of Certified Planners
1776 Massachusetts Avenue NW, #400
Washington, DC 20036
(202) 872-0611
Web site: http://www.planning.org

American Nursery and Landscape Association
1000 Vermont Avenue NW, Suite 300
Washington, DC 20005
(202) 789-2900
Web site: http://www.anla.org

American Society of Agronomy
677 South Segoe Road
Madison, WI 53711
(608) 273-8080
Web site: http://www.Agronomy.org

American Society of Landscape Architects
908 North Second Street
Harrisburg, PA 17102
(717) 236-2044
Web site: http://www.landscapearchitects.org

Associated Landscape Contractors of America (ALCA)
150 Elden Street, Suite 270
Herndon, VA 20170
(703) 736-9666
Web site: http://www.alca.org

Canadian Nursery Landscape Association
RR #4, Station Main
7856 Fifth Line S.
Milton, ON L9T2X8
Canada
(905) 875-1399
Web site: http://www.canadiannursery.com

Golf Course Superintendents Association of America
1421 Research Park Drive
Lawrence, KS 66049
(800) 472-7878
(785) 841-2240
Web site: http://www.gcsaa.org

Landscape Contractors Association of MD-DC-VA
15245 Shady Grove Road, Suite 130
Rockville, MD 20850
(301) 948-0810
Web site: http://www.lcamddcva.org

Landscape Maintenance Association (Florida)
P.O. Box 2035
Pace, FL 32571
(850) 994-3181
Web site: http://www.floridalma.org

National Institute on Park and Grounds Management
P.O. Box 5162
De Pere, WI 54115-5162
(920) 339-9057
Web site: http://www.nipgm.org

National Landscape Association
1000 Vermont Avenue NW, Suite 300
Washington, DC 20005
(202) 789-2900
Web site: http://www.anla.org

National Recreation and Park Association (NRPA)
22377 Belmont Ridge Road
Ashburn, VA 20148
(800) 626-6772
(703) 858-0784
Web site: http://www.nrpa.org

Professional Grounds Management Society (PGMS)
720 Light Street
Baltimore, MD 21230
(800) 609-7467
Web site: http://www.pgms.org

Professional Lawn Care Association of America (PLCAA)
1000 Johnson Ferry Road NE, Suite C-135
Marietta, GA 30068
(800) 458-3466
(770) 977-5222
Web site: http://www.plcaa.org

Sports Turf Managers Association
1027 South Third Street
Council Bluffs, IA 51503
(800) 323-3875
(712) 322-7862
Web site: http://www.sportsturfmanager.com

WEB SITES

Career Connections Training/Online Horticulture & Landscape Design Courses
http://www.career-connections.bc.ca/garden.htm

Groundskeeper University
http://www.groundskeeper.com

Landscape Online
http://www.landscapeonline.com

BOOKS

Buchanan, Rita. *Taylor's Master Guide to Landscaping*. Boston, MA: Houghton Mifflin, 2000.

Dell, Owen E. *How to Start a Home-Based Landscaping Business.* 2nd ed. Guilford, CT: Globe Pequot Press, 1997.

Erler, Catriona Tudor. *Complete Home Landscaping*. Saddle River, NJ: Creative Homeowner, 2000.

Gilman, Dr. Edward E. *An Illustrated Guide to Pruning.* Florence, KY: Delmar Publishers, 1997.

Gilman, Dr. Edward E. *Trees for Urban and Suburban Landscapes.* Florence, KY: Delmar Publishers, 1997.

Haegele, Katie. *Cool Careers Without College for Nature Lovers.* New York: The Rosen Publishing Group, Inc., 2000.

Taylor, Norman. *Taylor's Guide to Annuals*. Boston, MA: Houghton Mifflin, 2000.

Taylor, Norman. *Taylor's Guide to Ornamental Grasses*. Boston, MA: Houghton Mifflin, 1997.

Von Trapp, Sara Jane. *Landscaping from the Ground Up*. Newtown, CT: Taunton Press, 1997.

PERIODICALS

Golf Course Management
Golf Course Superintendents Association of America
1421 Research Park Drive
Lawrence, KS 66049
(800) 472-7878
(785) 841-2240
Web site: http://www.gcsaa.org

Golf Course News
United Publications, Inc.
P.O. Box 997
102 Lafayette Street
Yarmouth, ME 04096
(207) 846-0600
Web site: http://www.golfcoursenews.com

Grounds Maintenance
P.O. Box 12914
Overland Park, KS 66282
(800) 441-0294
Web site: http://www.primediabusiness.com

Landscape Management: Solutions for a Growing Industry
7500 Old Oak Boulevard
Cleveland, OH 44130
(440) 891-2729
Web site: http://www.landscapemanagement.net

Landscape Trades
Landscape Ontario
7856 Fifth Line
RR #4, Station Main
Milton, ON L9T 2X8
Canada
(905) 875-1805
Web site: http://www.hort-trades.com

Lawn & Landscape **Magazine**
4012 Bridge Avenue
Cleveland, OH 44113
(216) 961-4130
Web site: http://www.lawnandlandscape.com

8

HORTICULTURAL WRITER

Do you like looking at plants and flowers, reading about them, and talking to people who work with them? Do you also have a passion for writing? As a horticultural writer, you can communicate what you learn about plants and flowers by writing books or articles for magazines, scientific journals, newsletters, and even Web sites.

Besides the sheer joy of writing about what you love, you'll know your work is helping readers create more beautiful or productive gardens.

Description

In their articles and books, horticultural writers explore various aspects of making things grow. Because readers need up-to-date information and there is so much to learn about plants, many writers specialize in one or a few areas. Some write about plants or about certain kinds of plants, like vegetables, fruits, herbs, or ornamentals. Others write about flowers, or more specifically about perennials or annuals. Some focus primarily on writing pieces about beautifying the landscape, while others concentrate on more technical topics like soil preservation, pesticides, or how to choose proper gardening tools.

Most horticultural writers work as self-employed freelancers, writing for newspapers, magazines, scientific or technical journals, and Web sites. They might also write shorter articles, known as copy, for the advertising, marketing, or public relations departments of companies

A small child marvels at a giant exotic flower grown in a greenhouse, one of several places horticultural writers might visit while researching articles or books.

involved in horticulture, like fertilizer, gardening, or seed companies. They might prepare brochures or fact sheets about new company products or important company developments. Some horticultural writers work full-time as staff writers for these companies, or as staff writers for newspapers, magazines, or journals.

Like any writing, horticultural writing involves research. You must enjoy learning new things and be prepared to do the hard work of gathering facts. Researching an article or book can take hours, days, and even weeks. You might need to interview people working in the field, like nursery owners, florists, or botanists. To be a good interviewer, you must be curious and have a pleasant personality that puts people at ease so they're willing to answer your questions and provide additional information. You must also be a good listener. Careful note-taking is important, but for longer or more complicated interviews, you must know how to use a tape recorder.

Once you've done the research, or legwork, for an article or book, you have to sit down and write it. Some writers prefer to create short pieces of about 800 to 3,000 words. Others prefer writing longer works, such as books, concentrating on a single subject and writing thousands of words over the course of one or more years. Whatever you write, you need the discipline to stay focused on your project until it's completed.

You will also need good time-management skills. All writers must meet deadlines. You have to calculate how long your research and writing will take and schedule your time to meet your manuscript's due date.

Horticultural writing, like any writing, involves long periods of working alone. Even if you're employed by a newspaper, magazine, or company, and interact with fellow workers, you'll still spend many hours alone at your computer, researching and writing. Freelance writers lead an even more solitary life. Most of their contact with editors or supervisors is by mail, phone, or e-mail.

Writers, first and foremost, are communicators. Above all, you need a good command of the English language, including grammar, vocabulary, and spelling. You must be able to write clearly, in language that is easy to understand.

Education and Training

In high school, take courses in English and writing as well as biology and botany. Learn about plants and flowers by cultivating a small garden at home or by working for a farmer, landscaper, or nursery operator on your afternoons and summers off. Read as much as possible about plants and flowers in magazines, in books, and on Web sites.

To get hands-on writing experience, work on your high school newspaper, newsletter, or Web site. Any kind of writing

Besides being good with language, a horticultural writer must have a genuine love of plants and other living, growing things that they want to share with other people.

will improve your research and writing skills. You can also suggest horticultural articles to the editor of your hometown newspaper.

Many full-time staff writing positions on magazines and journals require college degrees. However, if you can show samples of your writing, known as clippings, published in your school or local newspaper, you might be able to get your foot in the door. Freelance writers without college degrees can work for magazines, but they, too, need to show work samples to get assignments. If you're thinking about writing technical or scientific works, you'll need to get more specialized knowledge, either by working in the field or through courses.

Outlook

Writing is a very competitive field, and horticultural writing is one of the most competitive because there are fewer consumer magazines and journals on the subject. But, as interest in gardening continues to grow, and as more and more gardening Web sites are created, there will be a long-term demand for good horticultural writers.

Writing for consumer magazines is most competitive. More opportunities exist writing for trade and professional journals. Writers who can understand and write clearly about technical and scientific aspects of horticulture are at a premium.

Staff writers usually earn more than freelance writers and generally receive company benefits like medical insurance and paid vacation time. Annual earnings for freelance writers vary, ranging from $10,000 to $100,000 or more, depending on who you work for and how many assignments you complete in a year. Advertising, marketing, and public relations work generally pays the most. Large national magazines and journals generally pay more for articles than small community newspapers and regional magazines. Books often pay the least up front, but if your book sells well and your contract includes royalties, which are a percentage of the sales, you can do very well. Writing books also can help you establish a reputation as an expert in the field.

How to Publish Your First Magazine Article

Magazines are a good place to start your writing career because editors are always looking for interesting articles to publish. Here are a few tips for getting your first story into print:

- **Choose a Small Magazine**

  Most major national magazines in the horticultural field use experienced writers. But smaller or regional magazines are usually willing to give new writers a chance to "break in." These publications often rely on new writers because they cannot afford the higher rates that more established writers charge.

- **Come Up with a Timely Idea**

  To attract the attention of a magazine editor, you need good ideas. Look for ideas based on current trends, or on new gardening methods or tools. If you've just read, for instance, that more homeowners are planting roses, and you know a lot about rose cultivation, that could be a good idea to pitch to an editor.

- **Choose the Right Magazine**

  The right magazine for an idea is one that publishes similar kinds of articles. If you want to write a story about home gardening, send the idea to magazines that publish stories about home gardening. To learn more about what magazines publish and names of editors to contact, pick up a copy of *Writer's Market*.

- **Write a Good Query Letter**

  Writers usually send letters to editors, called query letters, explaining their ideas. In general, a query letter should be a page long and should include no more than two or three separate ideas. Write one or two paragraphs detailing each idea. Be sure that your spelling and grammar are perfect. Your query letter helps show editors that you are a good writer!

- **Explain Why You're the Best Person to Write the Article**

  If you want to write about tulips, and you spent the last few summers working for a tulip grower, mention that at the end of your query letter. If you want to write about the best plants to grow in the shade, and you've had experience in your home or community garden, mention that.

- **Include Writing Samples**

  If you've published articles before, even in the school newspaper or the local garden club newsletter, include copies, known as clippings or clips, in your package. If you don't have samples, be sure to write the best and most convincing query letter possible. Include a stamped and self-addressed envelope (SASE) so the editor can respond to you. Expect to receive an answer in one or two months. If you don't sell your first ideas, be patient and keep trying! Sooner or later, you'll get that first assignment.

FOR MORE INFORMATION

ASSOCIATIONS

Agricultural Communicators in Education (college and government)
University of Florida
Mowry Roads, Building 116
P.O. Box 110811
Gainesville, FL 32611
Web site: http://www.aceweb.org

Agricultural Relations Council (public relations/advertising)
c/o NAMA (National Agri-Marketing Association)
11020 King Street, Suite 205
Overland Park, KS 66210

(913) 491-6500
Web site: http://www.nama.org/arc

American Society of Journalists and Authors (ASJA)
1501 Broadway, Suite 302
New York, NY 10036
(212) 645-2368
Web site: http://www.asja.org

Editorial Freelancers Association
71 West 23rd Street, Suite 1910
New York, NY 10010
(212) 929-5400
Web site: http://www.THE-EFA.org

Garden Writers Association of America
10210 Leatherleaf Court
Manassas, VA 22111
(703) 251-1032
Web site: http://www.gwaa.org

National Agri-Marketing Association (marketing and advertising)
11020 King Street, Suite 205
Overland Park, KS 66207
(913) 491-6500
Web site: http://www.nama.org

National Newspaper Association
P.O. Box 7540
Columbia, MO 65205-7540
(800) 829-4NNA (4662)
Web site: http://www.nna.org

National Writers Union
113 University Place, 6th Floor
New York, NY 10003
(212) 254-0279
Web site: http://www.nwu.org

North American Agricultural Journalists
264 Cumberland Court
College Station, TX 77845
(979) 845-2872
Web site: http://naaj.tamu.edu/

WEB SITES

Books and Writing Online
http://www.interzone.com/Books/books.html

Bookwire
http://www.bookwire.com

Media Bistro
http://www.mediabistro.com

Writer's Digest
http://www.writersdigest.com

BOOKS

Bowker, R.R. *Literary Market Place*. New Providence, NJ: R.R. Bowker/Reed Publishing, published annually.

Cool, Lisa Collier. *How to Write Irresistible Query Letters*. Cincinnati, OH: Writer's Digest Books, 2002.

Herman, Jeff. *The Writer's Guide to Book Editors, Publishers & Literary Agents*. Roseville, CA: Prima Publishing, 2001.

Tedesco, Anthony, and Paul Tedesco. *Online Markets for Writers: Where and How to Sell Your Writing on the Internet*. New York: Owl Books/Henry Holt, 2000.

White, William C., and Donald N. Collins. *Opportunities in Farming and Agriculture Careers*. Lincolnwood, IL: VGM Career Horizons/NTC Publishing, 1997.

Writer's Market. Cincinnati, OH: *Writer's Digest Books,* published annually.

Zuk, Judith D., and Christopher Brickell. *American Horticultural Society A-Z Encyclopedia of Garden Plants.* New York: DK Publishing, 1997.

PERIODICALS

The American Gardener
American Horticultural Society
7931 East Boulevard Drive
Alexandria, VA 22308
(703) 768-5700
Web site: http://www.ahs.org

The Herb Companion
Herb Companion Press
243 East Fourth Street
Loveland, CO 80537
(970) 663-0831
Web site: http://www.discoverherbs.com

Horticulture
98 North Washington Street
Boston, MA 02114
(617) 742-5600
Web site: http://www.hortmag.com

Organic Gardening
Rodale Press
33 East Minor Street
Emmaus, PA 18098
(610) 967-8363
Web site: http://www.organicgardening.com

LANDSCAPER

For many people, working in the fresh air, maintaining lawns and plantings for yards, gardens, parks, and other green spaces is a dream come true. As a landscaper, you'll work long, hard days in all kinds of weather. You'll use hand tools like shovels, rakes, and pruners, operate power machinery, drive trucks and power mowers, and haul heavy loads. Being a landscaper is physically demanding, but you'll reap the satisfaction of knowing you've beautified and improved the natural surroundings.

Description

Landscapers work outdoors, maintaining lawns and gardens at private homes and estates as well as green spaces at schools, office buildings, and shopping malls, and in parks, botanical gardens, arboretums, and cemeteries. The basic work includes seeding; fertilizing and mowing lawns; raking leaves and cleaning up outdoor areas; planting flowers, shrubs, and trees; trimming hedges; and pruning shrubs and trees.

Landscapers might also suggest certain types of plants and trees, as a nursery grower might. But landscapers' knowledge is usually not as extensive as that of landscape designers, or of landscape architects, who have four-year college degrees or master's degrees and are familiar with hundreds of different plants, flowers, shrubs, and trees, including exotic species.

Some landscapers also build brick or stone garden paths, install outdoor lighting and lawn sprinkler systems, erect fences, and build simple stone or brick walls. For complicated wall and drainage projects, however, most people turn to a landscape contractor.

These landscaping students work together to plant a tree in Mobara, Japan. Landscapers can work in cities, in suburbs, at the seaside, and in deserts.

Like many agricultural and horticultural workers, the work of a landscaper is physically challenging. Landscapers work almost exclusively outdoors, in weather extremes that range from blistering heat to freezing cold. The job involves a lot of walking, bending, and stretching. Landscapers have to use hand tools like shovels, rakes, and pruners, as well as power tools such as riding mowers, hedge trimmers, and chain saws. For big earth-moving projects, landscapers use large vehicles like dump trucks and backhoes.

Landscapers often are self-employed. They may work alone or with a partner. If they have many clients or very large projects, such as parks or arboretums, they may hire a crew of workers.

Some landscapers are employed by large landscaping firms. Others are employed by local or state municipalities and nonprofit organizations to work in public parks, cemeteries, botanical gardens, and arboretums. Some work for private companies that manage office buildings or hotels and resorts.

In addition to hands-on maintenance work, landscapers often inspect the grounds, provide written cost estimates for labor and materials, and send bills to clients. In a large company, the landscape supervisor usually handles these paperwork tasks. If you have good communications skills, you'll find it easier to attract new clients and to explain projects to them.

Education and Training

In high school, take courses in mathematics, the natural sciences (biology, botany, chemistry), communications, and business. If possible, attend a vocational high school that offers landscaping and horticulture courses.

Experience is the best teacher. After school, or on your summers off, work for a landscaper or landscaping firm.

Over a hundred years were spent building Butchart Gardens near Victoria, British Columbia. The gardens started out as an abandoned rock quarry.

Tools of the Trade

Landscapers use a variety of tools in their day-to-day work. Here are some of them:

Backhoe A vehicle with a large bucket attached on a movable arm that's used to dig holes and move soil and rocks from a landscaping site.

Bulb planter A metal or wood tool that makes holes in the earth in the proper size and depth for planting bulbs. Flowers grown from bulbs include tulips, daffodils, hyacinths, and lilies.

Chain saw A hand-held electric or gas-powered saw used to cut down trees or branches.

Garden spade A common hand-held implement that's similar to a shovel, but has a square blade and is used for digging holes.

Plumb line A string or cord used to assure that walls and fences are erected at the proper heights or angles.

Rake A common hand-held implement, including a fan-shaped garden type, with metal or bamboo prongs, or tines, used to gather leaves. A metal rake is used to level soil.

Roller A large machine with a rolling metal cylinder used to level soil or turf (grass).

Rototiller A compact power machine with rotating blades that turn over the soil in preparation for planting.

Shovel A common hand-held implement used to dig large holes or move materials like soil or rocks.

Stump grinder A power machine that grinds down stumps after trees have been cut and removed.

Weed trimmer Also known as a weed whacker, this hand-held electric or gas-powered machine is used to trim hedges, cut down brush, or trim grass along the edges of a plot of land.

You'll learn the most working for a full-service landscaper or firm that also performs simple landscape-design tasks like building garden paths and walls and installing outdoor lighting, as well as mowing lawns, trimming hedges, and performing clean-up duties.

While working, consider taking landscaping courses or specialized courses in arboriculture, horticulture, turf management, and landscape design at a community or junior college, or an agricultural college. These courses can help you get a head start on opening your own business, or allow you to move more quickly into a management position at a large landscaping firm.

Outlook

Landscaping jobs are expected to increase about as fast as the average for all other occupations through 2005. Most jobs are found in urban and suburban areas across the United States where there are large open spaces and a lot of new construction sites.

Annual salaries for landscapers range from about $23,000 to $60,000. Managers and supervisors for large landscaping firms earn at the higher end of the range, or more. Owners of landscaping businesses may also earn more, depending on the number of clients and whether those clients are residential or business customers. In general, business projects are larger and can pay more than residential customers.

FOR MORE INFORMATION

ASSOCIATIONS
American Nursery and Landscape Association
1000 Vermont Avenue NW, Suite 300
Washington, DC 20005
(202) 789-2900
Web site: http://www.anla.org

Associated Landscape Contractors of America (ALCA)
150 Elden Street, Suite 270
Herndon, VA 20170
(703) 736-9666
Web site: http://www.alca.org

Canadian Nursery Landscape Association
7856 Fifth Line S.
RR #4, Station Main
Milton, ON L9T 2X8
Canada
(905) 875-1399
Web site: http://www.canadiannursery.com

Landscape Contractors Association of MD-DC-VA
15245 Shady Grove Road, Suite 130
Rockville, MD 20850
(301) 948-0810
Web site: http://www.camddcva.org

Landscape Maintenance Association (Florida)
P.O. Box 2035
Pace, FL 32571
(850) 994-3181
Web site: http://www.floridalma.org

Professional Lawn Care Association of America (PLCAA)
1000 Johnson Ferry Road NE, Suite C-135
Marietta, GA 30068
(800) 458-3466
(770) 977-5222
Web site: http://www.plcaa.org

WEB SITES

Career Connections Training/Online Horticulture & Landscape Design Courses
http://www.career-connections.bc.ca/garden.htm

Landscape Online
http://www.landscapeonline.com

Urban Forest: 50 Careers in Trees
http://www.urbanforest.org

BOOKS

Buchanan, Rita. *Taylor's Master Guide to Landscaping.* Boston, MA: Houghton Mifflin, 2000.

Dell, Owen E. *How to Start a Home-Based Landscaping Business.* 2nd ed. Guilford, CT: Globe Pequot Press, 1997.

Erler, Catriona Tudor. *Complete Home Landscaping.* Saddle River, NJ: Creative Homeowner, 2000.

Gilman, Dr. Edward E. *An Illustrated Guide to Pruning.* Florence, KY: Delmar Publishers, 1997.

Gilman, Dr. Edward E. *Trees for Urban and Suburban Landscapes.* Florence, KY: Delmar Publishers, 1997.

Taylor, Norman. *Taylor's Guide to Annuals.* Boston, MA: Houghton Mifflin, 2000.

Taylor, Norman. *Taylor's Guide to Ornamental Grasses.* Boston, MA: Houghton Mifflin, 1997.

Von Trapp, Sara Jane. *Landscaping from the Ground Up.* Newtown, CT: Taunton Press, 1997.

PERIODICALS

Grounds Maintenance
P.O. Box 12914
Overland Park, KS 66282
(800) 441-0294
Web site: http://www.primediabusiness.com

cool climates work in winter, planning for the upcoming spring and summer growing seasons, planting seedlings, and repairing equipment.

Working as a nursery grower is fun, but it is also physically demanding. Some plants must be grown in greenhouses, which are usually very hot and humid. Most work is done outdoors in all kinds of weather, starting in the early morning with watering, weeding, and fertilizing. Throughout the day, there's a lot of bending, digging, stretching, and lifting of plant containers and equipment. Nursery growers and workers may have to load and unload shipments of trees and shrubs, transport heavy bags of potting soil and manure, carry large plantings to customers' cars, and make deliveries to customers' homes.

Nursery growers must know all about plants and how they grow so they can choose the best plants to sell in their regions, produce healthy specimens, and advise customers on plant selection and care. They have to know how to use and maintain greenhouses as well as basic gardening tools like rakes, shovels, and hoes.

Because retail nursery growers and workers have so much contact with the public, they must have good communications skills. If you're planning to open your own nursery, you also have to know how to price plantings, keep books, keep track of inventory, and manage nursery workers.

A refugee from Guatemala plants seedlings in a United Nations reforestation nursery. Working in a nursery will allow this man to observe the way that plants grow in a controlled environment.

Education and Training

Many nursery growers learn on the job, starting as entry-level nursery workers, or laborers, for small retail operations, and progressing to positions as managers or becoming nursery operators for their own businesses. It's helpful to take high-school courses in science, mathematics, and business, and to read as much as possible about plants, trees, and flowers. To gain valuable experience, work at a nursery on weekends, after school, or on your summers off.

Many nursery growers and laborers for wholesale operations have some post–secondary school training, usually a two-year degree from an agricultural college. For a management position in a large wholesale nursery operation, a two-year degree is usually necessary.

Salary

Retail nursery workers are usually paid an hourly wage of $5.50 to $15, depending on the size of the operation. Average salaries for managers range from $12,000 to $25,000 a year. Retail nursery operators and owners of large wholesale nurseries can earn considerably more, depending on the number and type of clients.

Outlook

Good growth is expected to continue for nursery workers as consumers continue to appreciate the beauty of gardens and plantings. Though nursery operators and managers usually work full-time throughout the year, in regions with short growing seasons, nursery workers, or laborers, may be employed only during the busy spring and summer seasons and at Christmastime.

FOR MORE INFORMATION

ASSOCIATIONS

American Nursery and Landscape Association
1000 Vermont Avenue NW, Suite 300
Washington, DC 20005
(202) 789-2900
Web site: http://www.anla.org

American Society for Horticultural Science
113 South West Street, Suite 200
Alexandria, VA 22314
(703) 836-4606
Web site: http://www.ashs.org

Professional Plant Growers Association
P.O. Box 27517
Lansing, MI 48909
(517) 694-7700

WEB SITES

Career Connections Training/Online Horticulture & Landscape Design Courses
http://www.career-connections.bc.ca/garden.htm

BOOKS

Cutler, Karen Davis, and Janet Marinelli, eds. *Starting from Seed: The Natural Gardener's Guide to Propagating Plants.* New York: Brooklyn Botanic Garden, 1998.

Dirr, Michael A. *Dirr's Hardy Trees and Shrubs: An Illustrated Encyclopedia*. Portland, OR: Timber Press, 1997.

Dirr, Michael A. *Manual of Woody Landscape Plants.* Champaign, IL: Stipes Publishing, 1998.

Gilman, Dr. Edward E. *Trees for Urban and Suburban Landscapes.* Florence, KY: Delmar Publishers, 1997.

Still, Steven. *Manual of Herbaceous Ornamental Plants*. Champaign, IL: Stipes Publishing, 1993.

Taylor, Norman. *Taylor's Guide to Annuals*. Boston, MA: Houghton Mifflin, 2000.

Taylor, Norman. *Taylor's Guide to Ornamental Grasses.* Boston, MA: Houghton Mifflin, 1997.

Zuk, Judith D., and Christopher Brickell. *American Horticultural Society A–Z Encyclopedia of Garden Plants*. New York: DK Publishing, 1997.

PERIODICALS

Digger
Oregon Association of Nurserymen
2780 SE Harrison, Suite 102
Milwaukie, OR 97222
(503) 653-8733
Web site: http://www.nurseryguide.com

GrowerTalks
Ball Publishing
335 North River Street
P.O. Box 9
Batavia, IL 60510
(630) 208-9080
Web site: http://www.growertalks.com

The Growing Edge
New Moon Publishing, Inc.
341 SW Second Street
Corvallis, OR 97333
(541) 757-2511
Web site: http://www.growingedge.com

Landscape Trades
Landscape Ontario
RR #4, Station Main
7856 Fifth Line South
Milton, ON L9T 2X8
Canada
(905) 875-1805
Web site: http://www.hort-trades.com

11

ORGANIC FARMER

Farmers have been around for centuries. With today's emphasis on healthy lifestyles, this earthy career has a new focus. Organic farmers grow fruits, vegetables, grains, herbs, and even flowers without using harmful pesticides and fertilizers. Beyond the joy of working outdoors and watching their crops grow, organic farmers

Organic farming produces food without harmful pesticides, chemicals, or genetic manipulation. These red worms are used to convert hog waste into fertilizer naturally.

help preserve the environment by keeping our water and soil clean and free of contaminants. They also help people live longer, healthier lives by providing all-natural food sources that are as free as possible of harmful chemicals.

Description

Like all farmers, organic farmers must enjoy working outdoors in all weather conditions. Work days are often long. In fact, half of all full-time farmers and farmworkers toil sixty or more hours a week. Because organic farmers usually use few machines or power tools in their work, organic farming can be even more labor intensive than traditional farming. Like all farmers, they do planting and cultivation in early spring and throughout summer, but they have to work in other seasons, too. In fall, they must harvest the summer crops, sow seeds for fall crops, and begin preparing the fields for spring planting. In winter, organic farmers continue preparation for the upcoming growing season by starting crops in greenhouses, and making repairs to barns, fences, and farm equipment.

Organic farmers, like traditional farmers, may work on a "diversified farm," which grows a variety of crops, including fruits, vegetables, herbs, and flowers. Many of them, however, concentrate on only one or two specialty crops, a growing trend in farming. For organic farmers, growing only one or two crops allows them to focus their energies carefully. Some organic farmers only grow vegetables. For them, there's nothing like the satisfaction of watching tomatoes swell from tiny pea-like orbs to big shiny red globes, or watching rows of corn rise along the landscape. Other organic farmers only grow grains like wheat or rye. Some grow flowers. For them, tending field upon field of tulips, daffodils, or other flowers is the ultimate outdoor experience. Some grow herbs for culinary, medicinal and decorative use.

What sets organic farmers apart from traditional farmers are their growing methods. Instead of using chemical

An Organic Farmer's Lexicon

acre An area measuring 43,560 square feet.

amendment A natural substance added to the soil to improve, or "amend," it.

compost Decaying plant or vegetable material used as a natural plant fertilizer.

crop rotation Alternating crops planted in the same ground from year to year to protect the soil's quality.

guano Droppings from animals, usually seabirds and bats, used as organic fertilizer.

manure The droppings of plant-eating animals, such as cows and horses, added to the soil to improve plant growth.

oilseed crops The name given to crops used in producing cooking oils, such as canola, soybeans, and sunflower seeds.

organic Relating to food or the production of food grown using all-natural plant or animal substances.

fertilizers, which can be harmful to soil and water, they concentrate on improving the soil, adding cow manure and other natural "amendments" that provide life-giving nutrients to crops. Fertilizers are made of natural substances that come from plants or animals. Rather than use chemical pesticides, organic farmers take preventative measures, using natural substances to grow healthy plants that are more resistant to insect infestation or disease. Some organic farmers also help protect the environment by using more hand tools, rather than machinery and power tools that consume polluting energy resources like gas and electricity.

Organic farmers are found throughout the United States. Where farmers live usually determines the crops they grow. That's especially true for organic farmers who insist on growing crops in the most natural way possible, never forcing them to grow in improper weather conditions.

Because many organic farmers grow only one or two crops, they often work on smaller farms, some as small as 10 acres. But it's not uncommon for them to join organic farming cooperatives—groups of organic farmers who join together to sell their harvested crops as well as share their knowledge about the latest methods for growing crops naturally.

Education and Training

In high school, take courses in agriculture, science, and mathematics. Attend a vocational high school, if possible,

and take agriculture courses. If you intend to start your own farm, take business courses. Join your local 4-H Club or a chapter of the national FFA (formerly known as Future Farmers of America). Pursuing a two-year degree at an agricultural college is not necessary, but can give you specialized knowledge in farming or, specifically, in organic farming.

The best way to learn about natural methods of cultivation is to work on an organic farm. Many organic farmers believe passionately in growing natural food sources and protecting the environment. To get the word out to others, some offer on-site courses or live-in internships for a small fee or in exchange for your labor.

Outlook

Overall, the number of U.S. farms is expected to continue declining through 2010. This is because smaller farms are being consolidated into larger agricultural concerns often owned by large corporations. But even these larger farms will need farmhands.

At the same time, small specialty farms that grow a particular crop are on the increase. With Americans' growing

On organic farms and in organic greenhouses, crops are often planted in such a way as to preserve soil nutrients, allowing the same patch of ground to be used countless times.

interest in healthy, unadulterated foods, there should be a rising demand for organic farmers who work on, manage, or own small specialty farms.

Salaries for farmers vary greatly, from $20,000 to as much as $100,000 a year, depending on whether they work on a large or small farm, the kinds of crops they grow, and to whom they supply their products. As a beginning farmworker, or laborer, you can expect to earn about $11,000. An experienced farm manager can earn $40,000 to $140,000 or more.

FOR MORE INFORMATION

ASSOCIATIONS

American Farm Bureau Federation
225 Touhy Avenue
Park Ridge, IL 60068
(847) 685-8896
Web site: http://www.fb.org

Biodynamic Farming and Gardening Association
Thoreau Center, Building 1002B
The Presidio
P.O. Box 29135
San Francisco, CA 94129
(888) 516-7797
Web site: http://www.biodynamics.com

Canadian Organic Growers
P.O. Box 6408
Station J
Ottawa, ON K2A 3Y6
Canada
(613) 231-9047
Web site: http://www.cog.ca

4-H
Stop 2225
1400 Independence Avenue SW
Washington, DC 20205
(202) 720-2908
Web site: http://www.4h-usa.org

National FFA Organization (formerly known as Future Farmers of America)
6060 FFA Drive
P.O. Box 68960
Indianapolis, IN 46268
(317) 802-6060
Web site: http://www.ffa.org

National Young Farmer Educational Association
P.O. Box 20326
Montgomery, AL 36120
(334) 288-0097
Web site: http://www.nyfea.org

Organic Farming Research Foundation
P.O. Box 440
Santa Cruz, CA 95061
(831) 426-6606
Web site: http://www.ofrf.org

The Rodale Institute
611 Siegfriedale Road
Kutztown, PA 19530
(610) 683-1400
Web site: http://www.rodaleinstitute.org

U.S. Department of Agriculture (USDA)
Higher Education Program
14th Street and Independence SW
Washington, DC 20250
(202) 720-2791
Web site: http://www.usda.org

WEB SITES

Do Not Panic, Eat Organic
http://www.rain.org

Global Resource for Organic Information
http://www.allorganiclinks.org

Greentrade: The Reference for Organic Farming Professionals
http://www.greentrade.net

International Willing Workers on Organic Farms (Volunteer Opportunities)
http://www.wwoof.org
http://www.organicvolunteers.com

Northeast Organic Farming Association of Vermont
http://www.nofavt.org

BOOKS

Byczynski, Lynn. *The Flower Farmer: An Organic Grower's Guide to Raising and Selling Cut Flowers.* White River Junction, VT: Chelsea Green Publishing, 1997.

Coleman, Eliot, and Chelsea Green, eds. *The New Organic Grower: A Master's Manual of Tools and Techniques for the Home and Market Gardener.* White River Junction, VT: Chelsea Green Publishing, 1995.

Langer, Richard W. *Grow It! The Beginner's Guide to a Complete in-Harmony-with-Nature Small Farm.* New York: Farrar, Straus & Giroux, 1994.

Smillie, Joe, and Grace Gershung. *The Soul of Soil: A Soil-Building Guide for Gardeners and Farmers*. White River Junction, VT: Chelsea Green Publishing, 1999.

PERIODICALS

The Herb Companion
Herb Companion Press
243 East Fourth Street
Loveland, CO 80537
(970) 663-0831
Web site: http://www.discoverherbs.com

Organic Gardening
Rodale Press
33 East Minor St.
Emmaus, PA 18098
(610) 967-8363
Web site: http://www.organicgardening.com

Progressive Farmer
P.O. Box 830656
Birmingham, AL 35283
(800) 292-2340
Web site: http://www.progressivefarmer.com

12

SOIL CONSERVATION TECHNICIAN

Who says dirt is worthless? To farmers and planters, soil is pure gold. Good quality soil enables them to grow valuable food crops as well as trees, plants, and flowers. Clean water is also essential to plant growth. But when soil is depleted of important nutrients and water becomes polluted, crops fail. As a soil conservation technician, you partici-pate in the growing process at ground level, helping maintain soil and water quality for future generations of farmers and foresters.

Description

Soil conservation technicians help protect the environment by conserving land and water. They reclaim and restore soil and water to increase crop yields as well as to preserve wildlife. Out in the field, they collect soil samples, make notes, and map problem areas. They perform engineering surveys and work directly with farmers and other land users to help design and implement irrigation and drainage systems, terraces, grassed waterways, and other projects to protect valuable soil from erosion. They closely monitor land-use projects to insure their practices are working.

Most soil conservation technicians work for the federal government. They assist conservationists and engineers in agencies like the Soil Conservation Service, the U.S. Bureau of Land Management, and the U.S. Bureau of Federal Reclamation. Many other soil conservation technicians do similar work for county and state governments. Other soil conservation technicians work for private companies like public utilities, banks and loan agencies, and mining and steel companies.

There are many kinds of soil conservation technicians. Physical science technician aides are out in the field, studying the soil, gathering data, and mapping land. Range technicians

A soil conservation specialist talks with a farmer about the moisture levels in his soil. If soil does not receive enough rainwater or is not properly irrigated, it will be difficult to grow anything in it.

gather data and assess erosion hazards for the country's rangelands where cattle and other animals graze. Surveying technicians map out fields and lay out construction. Engineering technician aides measure acreage, conduct field tests, and help construct dams and irrigation projects. Cartographic survey technicians work with mapmakers to survey public lands, identify prominent land features, and help determine the best use of land.

Soil conservation technicians generally work about forty hours a week, though they may work longer days if there's a natural disaster, such as a hurricane or flood. They spend much of their time outdoors in the field, often on farms. Although they usually drive to work sites, they often walk great distances. They may travel long distances. Part of their time is spent indoors, preparing written surveys and studies.

Soil conservation technicians have to be familiar with water and soil. They must also understand mapping techniques and know how to use surveying instruments and other technical tools of the trade.

Although working as a soil conservation technician is a hands-on job, you'll also need to be a good communicator. You'll have to enjoy writing and using computers since you'll have to write clear reports on your data and tests. You'll also have a lot of contact with other people. You have to be friendly and be able to speak clearly. You'll work closely with conservationists and engineers, explaining your surveys and findings and helping to lay out and build land-reclamation projects. You'll also work closely with farmers and other land users as you explain complex problems and solutions in language they can easily understand.

Education and Training

While in high school, take courses in algebra, biology, earth sciences, English (including writing), and computers. If you

Improper farming techniques can turn rich topsoil into dry, sandy soil. This is one of the effects of poor soil conservation, and it can take years to reverse.

can, attend a vocational high school and take classes in agriculture. After school and during summers off, you can learn a lot about soil conservation by working on a farm. You can also join a 4-H Club or the National FFA Organization (formerly Future Farmers of America).

Upon graduation, many soil conservation technicians get on-the-job training. But jobs with government agencies are often based on an exam. To prepare for the exam and supplement your learning, consider taking soil conservation courses at a technical college. No certification, license, or college training is required for soil conservation technicians.

But to improve your job prospects, consider earning a certificate in soil science from the American Society of Agronomy or the Soil and Water Conservation Society. A two-year program at a technical institute can lead to work at the higher level of soil conservationist.

Salary

Salaries for soil conservation technicians who work for the federal government are set by government service rating. The policy of promoting from within allows soil conservation technicians to advance at a regular pace. Starting salaries for soil conservation technicians are about $15,500 to $20,000, depending on experience, education, and area of work.

Outlook

Jobs for soil conservation technicians are expected to increase about as fast as the average for other occupations. Since most jobs are with the federal government, much depends on increases or decreases in federal spending. However, if government spending for conservation decreases, jobs in state and local governments, at public utilities, banks and loan companies, and with mining and steel companies may increase to meet the all-important need for soil conservation.

Reclaiming the Dust

Preserving our soil and land resources is just plain common sense. But it was not until 1908 that President Theodore Roosevelt appointed the country's first National Conservation Commission to manage our natural resources.

However, the National Conservation Commission did not foresee the tragedy that would occur on many of our nation's farms only a few decades later.

During World War I, there was a shortage of wheat, and many Midwestern farmers began planting thousands of acres of wheat. Year after year, they planted wheat in the same soil. By the mid-1930s, the soil was dry and depleted of valuable nutrients. Dust storms across the plains carried away more than 800 million tons of topsoil! Many areas of the United States became like deserts, and farmers were unable to grow crops to feed their starving families.

Once again the federal government stepped in. In 1935, the Soil Conservation Service of the U.S. Department of Agriculture was established to help restore and reclaim valuable farmlands. They were aided by the Civilian Conservation Corps (CCC), created by President Franklin Roosevelt to help ease unemployment during the Great Depression. Their efforts were largely successful, and many farmers were able to reclaim their fields.

In the years since then, the federal government has established several thousand soil conservation districts across the United States. Their work will help insure that Americans never again lose their fields to dust.

FOR MORE INFORMATION

ASSOCIATIONS

American Society of Agronomy
Career Development and Placement Service
677 South Segoe Road
Madison, WI 53711
(608) 273-8080
Web site: http://www.agronomy.org

4-H
Stop 2225
1400 Independence Avenue SW
Washington, DC 20250
(202) 720-2908
Web site: http://www.4h-usa.org

National FFA Organization (formerly Future Farmers of America)
6060 FFA Drive
P.O. Box 68960
Indianapolis, IN 46268
(317) 802-6060
Web site: http://www.ffa.org

Natural Resources Conservation Service
U.S. Department of Agriculture
Attn: Conservation Communications Staff
P.O. Box 2890
Washington, DC 20013
Web site: http://www.nrcs.usda.gov

Soil and Water Conservation Society
7515 NE Ankeny Road
Ankeny, IA 50021
(515) 289-2331
Web site: http://www.swcs.org

Soil Science Society of America
677 South Segoe Road
Madison, WI 53711
(608) 273-8080
Web site: http://www.soils.org

BOOKS

Gregorich, E. G., et al., eds. *Soil and Environmental Science Dictionary*. New York: CRC Press, 2001.

Kohnke, Helmut, and D. P. Franzmeier. *Soil Science Simplified*. Prospect Heights, IL: Waveland Press, 1995.

Smillie, Joe, and Grace Gershung. *The Soul of Soil: A Soil-Building Guide for Gardeners and Farmers*. White River Junction, VT: Chelsea Green Publishing, 1999.

Thompkins, Peter, and Christopher Baird. *Secrets of the Soil: New Solutions for Restoring Our Planet*. Anchorage, AK: Earthpulse Press, 1998.

PERIODICALS

E: The Environmental Magazine
Earth Action Network
P.O. Box 5098
Westport, CT 06881
(203) 866-0602
Web site: http://www.emagazine.com

Environment
Heldref Publications
1319 18th Street NW
Washington, DC 20036
(202) 296-6267
Web site: http://www.heldref.org

Outdoor America
Isaak Walton League of America
707 Conservation Lane
Gaithersburg, MD 20878
(301) 548-0150
Web site: http://www.iwla.org

GLOSSARY

agribusiness The entire business of growing and selling crops, from planting and cultivation to processing, marketing, and sales.

agriculture The science and art of cultivating the soil and producing crops.

agronomy The branch of agriculture dealing with soil management and field-crop production.

arboretum A place where trees, shrubs, and woody plants are grown and displayed for scientific or educational purposes.

arboriculture The science of planting and cultivating trees.

boutonniere A flower or small bouquet created by a florist and worn in the buttonhole of a shirt or suit.

cartography The art and science of making maps.

contaminant A substance that poisons people, animals, or the environment.

culinary Something used in or related to cooking, such as a culinary herb.

dendrology The study of trees.

exotic Something that comes from a foreign place or is strikingly different or unusual.

floriculture The art and science of growing, marketing, and designing with flowers and plants.

grafting The technique of propagating or creating a new plant by tying a shoot from a new plant to an older, established plant.

herbicide A chemical or natural substance used to control or kill weeds.

horticulture The science and art of cultivating, propagating, processing, and marketing plants, flowers, turf, vegetables, fruits, and nuts.

irrigation The use of special methods or construction to supply water to dry lands.

land reclamation The process of restoring and reclaiming land that has been eroded or depleted of nutrients.

nutrient A mineral or other substance that nourishes.

ornamental A flower, plant, or tree cultivated for its beauty and decorative use rather than for a practical use such as food or fuel.

pesticide A chemical or natural substance used to control or kill insects; also called insecticide.

propagate To reproduce plants from already existing plants using cuttings, or techniques like grafting and tissue culture.

rangeland Land where cattle and other livestock graze on grasses and other plants.

soil depletion The process by which soil loses valuable nutrients needed for plant growth.

soil erosion The wearing away of soil by wind, water, or other natural forces.

INDEX

A
aerial photography, 9, 11, 13–15
agricultural aviation pilot, 8, 9–10
    dangers, 9–10, 13
    description, 10–13
    education and training, 13–15
    outlook, 15–16
    resources, 16–19
    salary, 15
Agriculture Research Service, 53
American Society of Agronomy, 131
American Society of Botanical Artists (ASBA),
    38, 39
arborist, 20–21
    dangers, 23
    description, 21–23

education and training, 23–25
outlook, 25
resources, 28–30
salary, 25
Associated Landscape Contractors
    of America (ALCA), 72

B
botanical artist, 8, 31–32
    description, 32–35
    education and training, 35–37,
        39
    outlook, 37
    profile, 38–39
    resources, 40–41
    salary, 38

C
chemical fertilizers, history of,
    14–15
Civilian Conservation Corps
    (CCC), 132–133
commercial pilot's license, 13
consulting arborist, 23

D
Dust Bowl, 132–133

F
farm crop production technician,
    42–43
    description, 43–46
    education and training, 46–47
    outlook, 47

resources, 48–49
salary, 47
farm equipment technician, 50–51
    description, 51–55
    education and training, 55
    outlook, 55–56
    resources, 56–58
    salary, 56
    types of, 53
farms, types of machines used
    on, 54
Federal Aviation Administration
    (FAA), 13
florist, 8, 59–60
    description, 60–62
    education and training, 62–65
    outlook, 65–66
    resources, 66–67
    salary, 65
flowers for decoration, history
    of, 63
4-H Club, 46, 121, 130
FTD, 62

G
Glaubner, J. R., 14
Great Depression, 133
greenskeeper, 69–70
groundskeeper, 8, 25, 68–69
    description, 69–72
    education and training, 72
    outlook, 72–73
    profile, 73–75
    resources, 76–80
    salary, 73

H

horticultural writer, 81–83
  description, 83–85
  education and training, 85–87
  how to publish first article,
    88–90
  outlook, 87
  resources, 90–93
  salary, 87

I

International Society of
  Arboriculture, 24

L

landscape designer/architect, 95
landscaper, 8, 94–95
  description, 95–97
  education and training, 97–101
  outlook, 102
  resources, 102–105
  salary, 102
  tools used by, 100–101
Lawes, John B., 15

N

National Conservation
  Commission, 132
National FFA Organization, 46,
  121, 130
nursery grower, 106–107
  description, 107–109
  education and training,
    110–111
  outlook, 111
  resources, 112–114
  salary, 111

O

organic farmer, 8, 115–116
  description, 116–119
  education and training,
    119–121
  outlook, 121–122
  resources, 122–125
  salary, 122
organic farming cooperatives,
  119

P

Professional Grounds Management
  Society (PGMS), 72

R

Roosevelt, President Franklin, 133
Roosevelt, President Theodore, 132

S

Soil and Water Conservation
  Society, 131
Soil Conservation Service, 127, 132
soil conservation technician,
  126–127
  description, 127–129
  education and training,
    129–131
  outlook, 131
  resources, 133–135

salary, 131
types of, 127–128

T
Tele-Flora, 62
trees, important functions of,
     26–27

U
U.S. Bureau of Federal
     Reclamation, 127

U.S. Bureau of Land
     Management, 127
U.S. Department of Agriculture,
     26, 53, 132
U.S. Forest Service, 26–27

W
Writer's Market, 89

About the Author

Monique Burns is a New York City freelance writer who operated The Flower Potter, a flower-box arranging business, in Rockport, Massachusetts.

Photo Credits

Cover © Michael S. Yamashita/Corbis; pp. 9, 10 © Joey Gardner/Salisbury *Daily Times*/AP/Wide World Photos; p. 12 © Brian Myrick/*Daytona Beach News-Journal*/ AP/Wide World Photos; pp. 20, 22 © *Journal-Courier*/ Steve Warmowski/The Image Works; p.24 © Frank Siteman/Index Stock Imagery, Inc.; pp. 31, 33 © Kelly Mooney Photography/Corbis; p. 36 © Cynthia Hart Designer/Corbis; pp. 42, 44, 50, 52 © Inga Spence/Index Stock Imagery, Inc.; p. 46 © Syracuse Newspapers/C.W. McKeen/The Image Works, Inc.; pp. 59, 61 © Benelux Press/Index Stock Imagery, Inc.; p. 64 © Tomas del Amo/Index Stock Imagery, Inc.; pp. 68, 70 © Kathy Willens/AP/Wide World Photos; p. 74 © Kevin R. Morris/ Corbis; pp. 81, 86 © Ariel Skelley/Corbis; p. 82 © AP/Wide World Photos; pp. 94, 96 © Michael S. Yamashita/Corbis; pp. 98–99 © The Image Bank; pp. 106, 108 © Bonnie Kamin/Index Stock Imagery, Inc.; p. 110 © Howard Davies/Corbis; pp. 115, 116 © David

Design and Layout

Evelyn Horovicz